# The Button Blanket
## AN ACTIVITY BOOK ages 6–10

A Northwest Coast Indian Art Series
**by Nan McNutt**

Design and Illustrations by
Upstream Productions
**Yasu Osawa**

Northwest Coast Art by
**Barry Scow**

ISBN 1-57061-118-1

**SASQUATCH BOOKS**
SEATTLE

In Memory of
Gla-Why-Agliss
Chief William Scow

Hereditary Chief of the Kwiksutianeuk Tribe
of the Kwakiutl Nation

## Acknowledgments

My deep gratitude goes to *Bill Holm* for his long-standing help and guidance, and to *Yasu Osawa* for his ability to see my vision and put it wonderfully down on paper.

A special thanks to *Nancy Dawson* for her dedication to the intent of this book as a teacher as well as an artist.

For their gracious assistance and editorial comments, I want to thank *Steve Brown, James Haggarty, Sadie Hinsberger, Marie James, Doreen Jensen, Shigeko Kaino, Carolyn Marr, Sharol Otness, Mary Reyes, Beatrice Scow* and *Jan and Kevin Shea.*

The elementary teachers of Petersburg, Alaska, played an especially important role in teaching these activities; thank you *Tracy Littleton (k), Rita Franzel (2nd), Dick Longworth (2nd), Sally Reimer (3rd), Melissa Carraway (Principal).*

A very special thanks to all their students who really worked on this book.

**Note for parents and teachers:**

While the actual cover of this book can be used for the main cut-and-paste activity, we have also included an extra full-color "cover insert" for the child's use, bound into the middle of the book to preserve the book's cover.

There was going to be a
celebration at the big house.
Ann would dance for the
first time.

*A*nn had danced before at home. She wore her baby blanket. Grandpa and Dad would sing. First Ann would turn gently one way. Then she would turn the other. That was how Mom and Grandma danced.

"There will be a celebration, a potlatch," said Grandma. "Some of our important people will receive Kwakiutl names. Some people, like you, will dance for the first time. Everyone will be at the big house. It's time you have a button blanket."

Ann dreamed about her new button blanket with a special crest. "But, who will make my special crest?" thought Ann.

At the store Mom bought some dark blue wool. It felt soft and warm to Ann. Mom also bought some bright red wool for Ann's special crest. "Will Uncle make my crest?" asked Ann.

Ann looked at buttons made from shells. She turned them in her fingers. The buttons felt smooth and cold. They sparkled with rainbow colors as she moved them. Then Ann counted 300 buttons for her button blanket.

When Mom and Ann got home, Grandma measured and cut the wool. It hung over Ann's shoulders. The sides of the wool touched her hands. Ann played with the wool between her fingers. She thought about dancing in her new button blanket.

"Now stand still!" said Grandma. She measured the wool.

Grandma smiled.
"Just right," she said.

Grandma sewed the red trim around three sides. Ann watched the needle go up, then down; up, then down.

"Will Uncle make my crest?" asked Ann.

Grandma stopped the sewing machine. "You'd better go and ask," Grandma said.

Ann found Uncle outside. He was carving a mask for the potlatch. He would wear it when he danced.

"How's your button blanket coming?" asked Uncle. He set his adze and mask down beside him.

"It needs my special crest," answered Ann. "Would you make my crest?"

"I thought you'd never ask," her Uncle smiled.

8.

With pencil and paper,
Uncle drew out the crest.

With pins and scissors, Mom
cut it out of red wool.

With needle and thread,
Grandma sewed the red
crest on the dark blue
blanket.

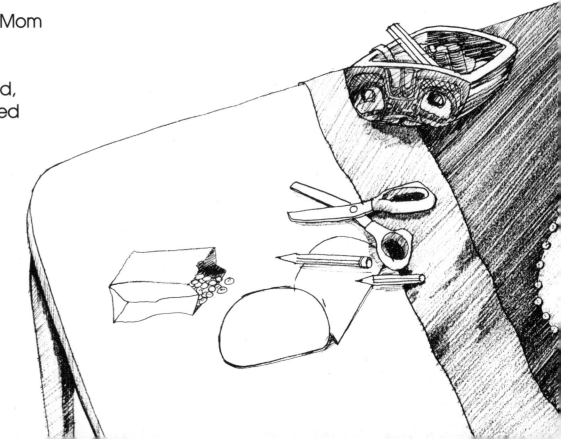

Then Ann pulled out the bag of 300 shiny buttons.

And, one by one Grandma helped her sew the buttons on her new button blanket.

The time for the potlatch finally came. Everyone was there. Grandpa, Grandma, Mom, Dad, Uncle and baby brother were at the big house too. And, Ann danced for the first time,

**W**hen Ann's Uncle drew her crest, she learned about two basic shapes in Northwest Coast Indian art. The first shape was the "U" form.

*YOU NEED:*

PASTE

SALT OR CORNMEAL

FIGURE

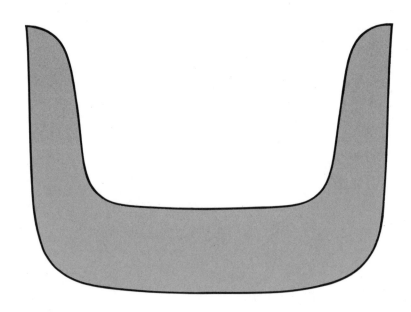

*DIRECTIONS:*

1. Spread paste on "U".

2. Sprinkle salt or cornmeal over "U".

3. Leave out to dry.

4. Shake off extra cornmeal or salt.

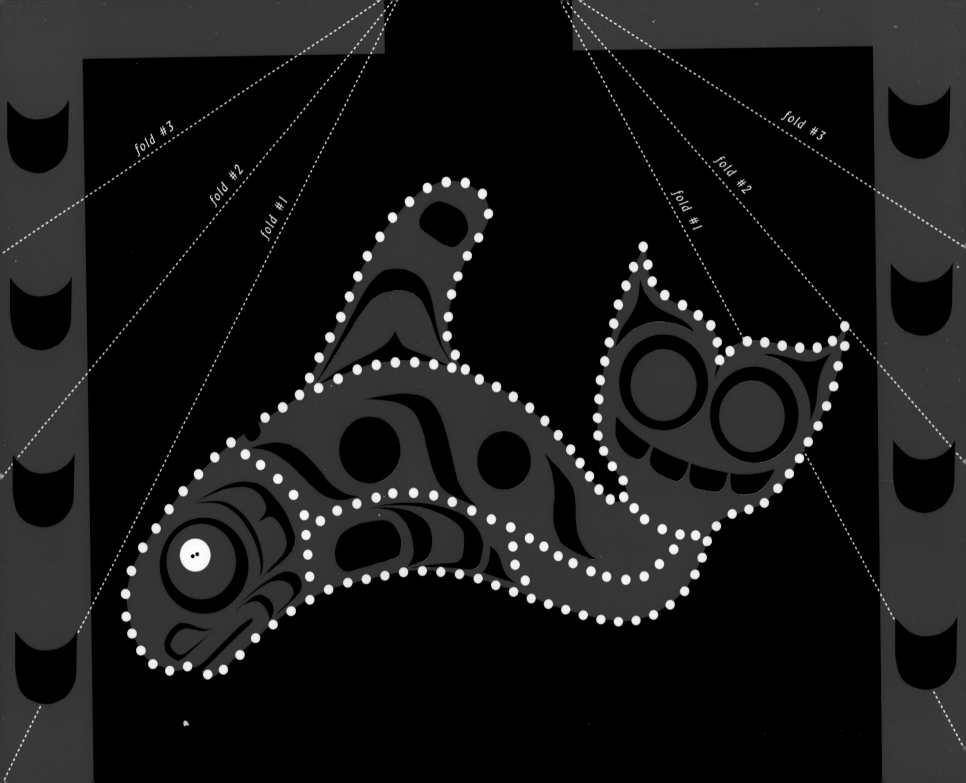

fold #3

fold #3

fold #2

fold #2

fold #1

fold #1

# *T*his is a **"U"** form

*YOU NEED:*

COLOR CRAYON

SCISSORS

*DIRECTIONS:*
1. Color the "U".
2. Cut the "U" out.
3. Save it!

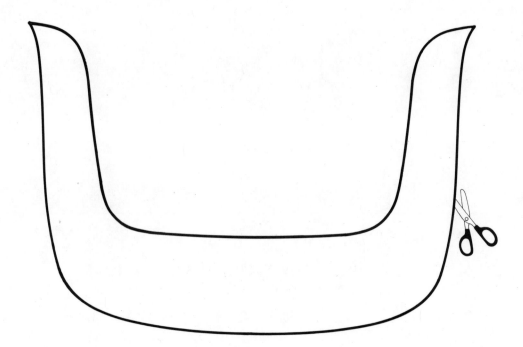

# Another "U"

## YOU NEED:

COLOR CRAYON

SCISSORS

## DIRECTIONS:

1. Color the "U".

2. Cut out one more "U".

Now, how many "U"s do you have?

16

# *A* stack of "U"s

PASTE

COLOR CRAYON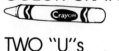

TWO "U"s

*DIRECTIONS:*

1. Match up the "U"s.

2. Paste them down.

3. Color the remaining "U"s.

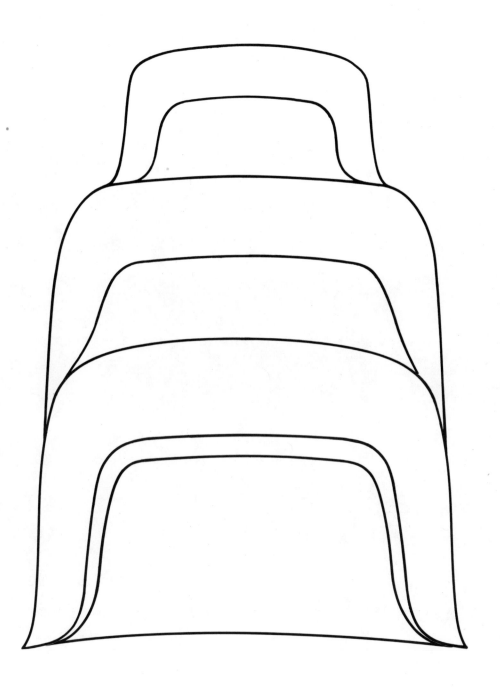

*T*he second shape Ann learned about from her Uncle was called an Ovoid. It looked like this.

*YOU NEED:*

PASTE

SALT OR CORNMEAL

FIGURE

*DIRECTIONS:*

1. Spread paste on Ovoid.
2. Sprinkle salt or cornmeal over it.
3. Leave out to dry.
4. Shake off extra salt or cornmeal.

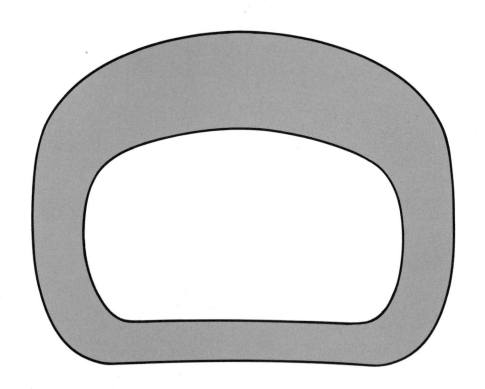

When Ovoid is dry, feel it.

# **W**hat does an **Ovoid** look like?

My answer: _____

*YOU NEED:*

COLOR CRAYONS

SCISSORS

*DIRECTIONS:*

1. Color the Ovoid.

2. Cut out the Ovoid.

3. Save it.

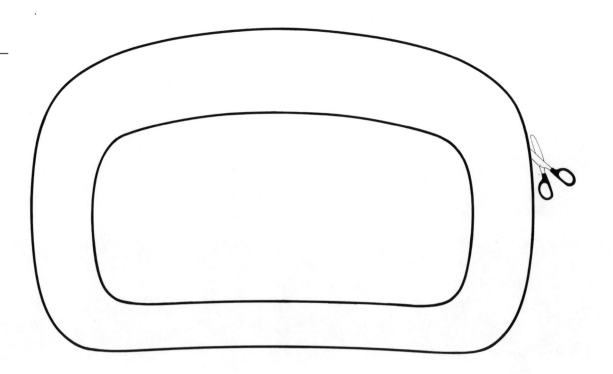

# *T*he Inside Piece.

This shape is an Inner Ovoid because it goes inside the larger Ovoid.

*YOU NEED:*

COLOR CRAYON

SCISSORS

*DIRECTIONS:*

1. Color the Inner Ovoid.

2. Cut it out.

3. Save it.

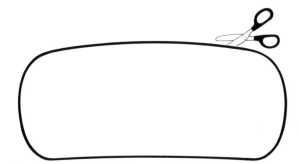

# *D*iving Whale's Tail

YOU NEED:

COLOR CRAYON

PASTE

ONE OVOID

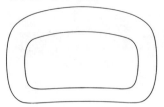

ONE INNER OVOID

*DIRECTIONS:*

1. Match up the pieces.

2. Paste them on.

3. Color the "U" forms.

# *B*utton Blanket Design: A Whale's Head

## WHAT YOU NEED:

DARK BLUE
CONSTRUCTION PAPER

WHALE'S HEAD

SCISSORS

LARGE 1" BUTTON

GLUE

cut

Place pieces
on blue paper.

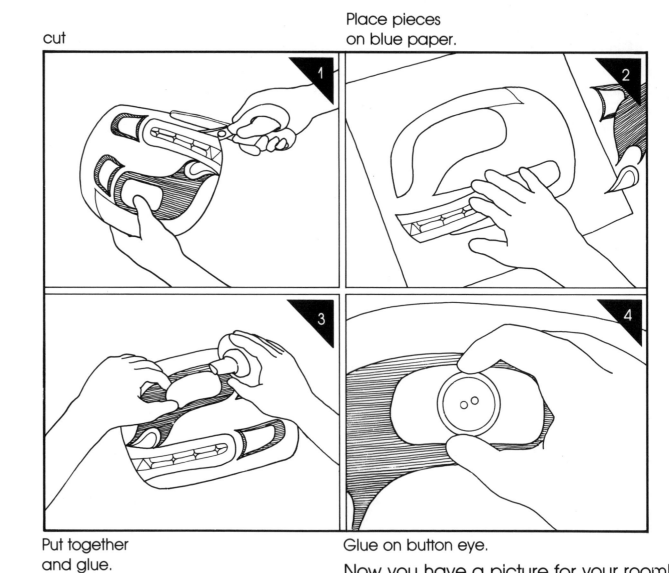

Put together
and glue.

Glue on button eye.

## Now you have a picture for your room!

If you want to sew on the
button, see instructions for
threading needle and button
on page 38.

# Whale's Head

**WHAT YOU NEED:**

RED COLOR CRAYONS

SCISSORS

**DIRECTIONS:**

1. Color the whale's head but not shaded parts.
2. Cut along the heavy line.
3. Throw away shaded parts
4. Now put the puzzle together.

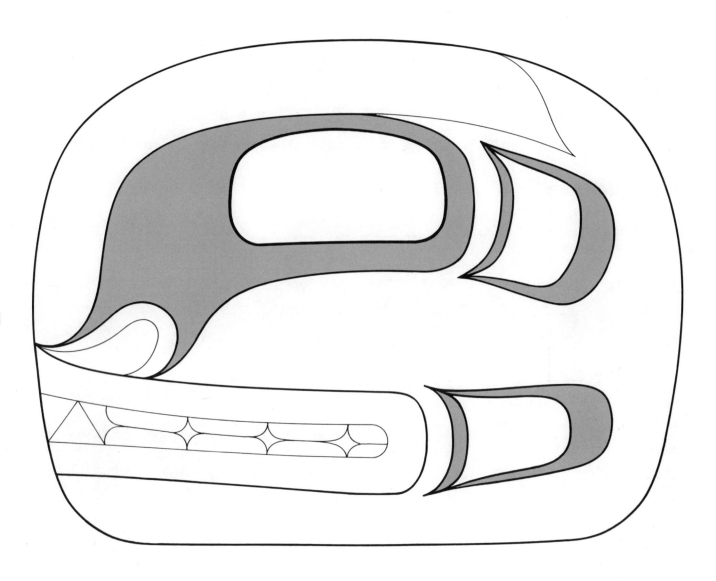

# *B*ody Parts
## of the Whale's Head

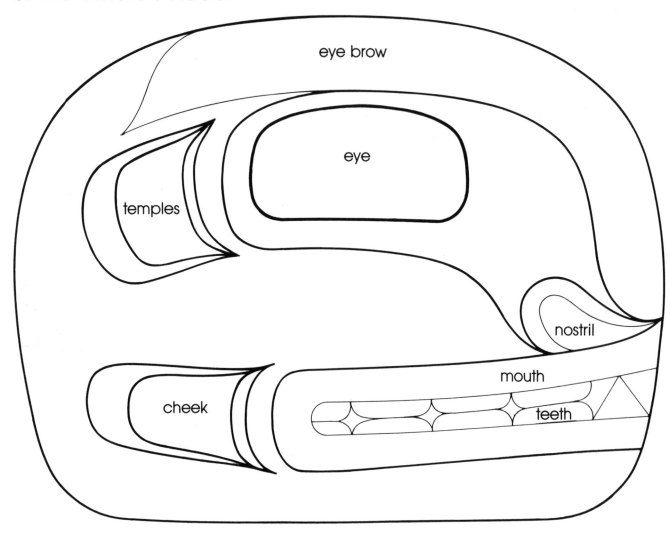

eye brow

eye

temples

nostril

mouth

cheek

teeth

# $A$ Button Blanket for your Paper Person

## WHAT YOU NEED:

### BOOK COVER OR COVER INSERT

### SCISSORS

cut

Fold #1

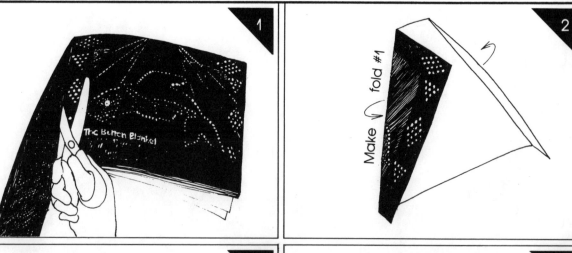

1

2

Make fold #1

3

4

Make fold #2

Make fold #2

Make fold #3 and fold other side
of Blanket

Hang button blanket
on paper person.

# Make a
## Dancing Paper Person

*WHAT YOU NEED:*

COLOR CRAYONS

SCISSORS

6" STRING

TAPE

PAPER CLIP

PAPER PERSON ON PAGES
27 or 28

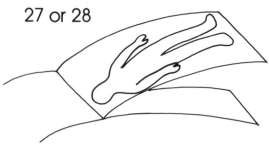

color                    cut

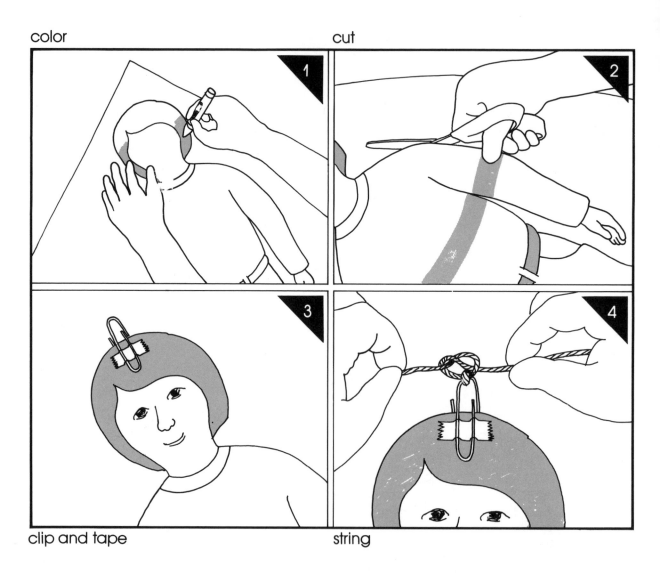

clip and tape            string

# Paper Person

Use this page *or* next page.

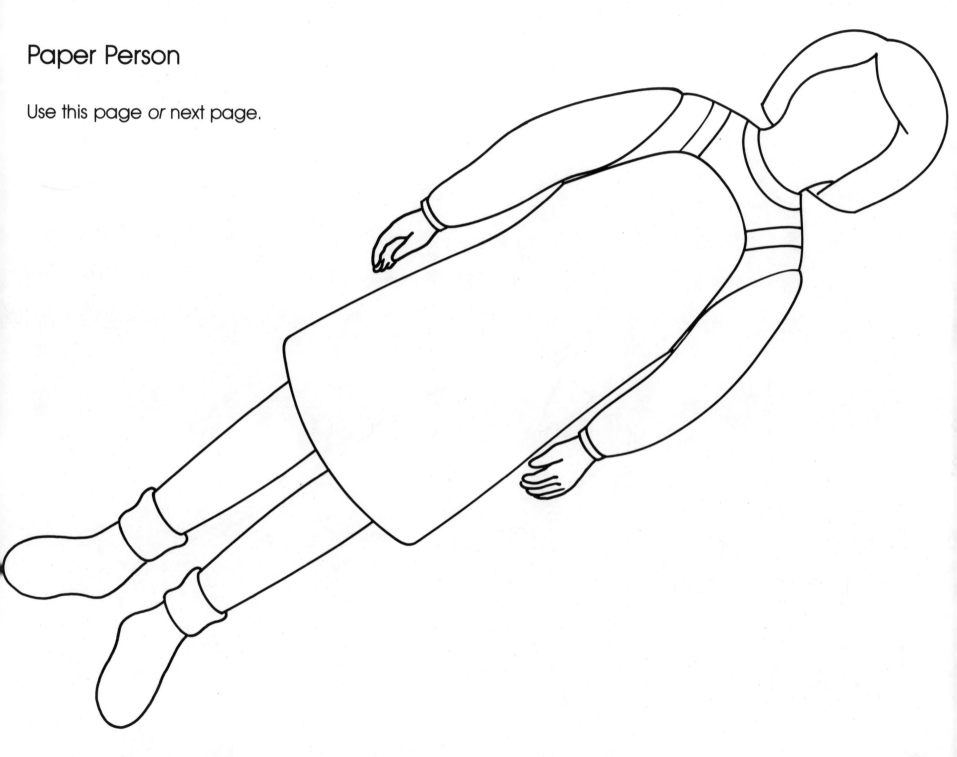

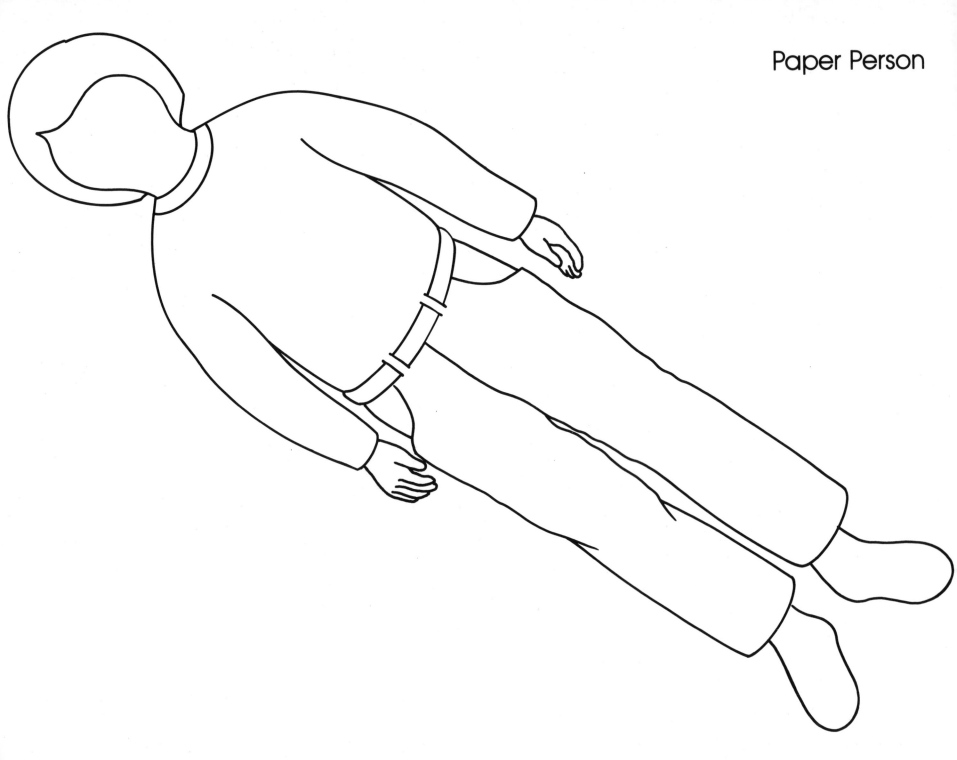

Paper Person

# The Button Blanket
ADULT TEACHING GUIDE

*T*he Button Blanket is the second in a four part series of activity books for children on **Northwest Coast Indian Art.** Although this book has been designed for children 5-9, if accompanied with the first book, **The Bentwood Box,** children 9-14 will be able to make button blanket designs and distinguish Kwakiutl art from Northern art forms: Tlingit, Haida, Tsimshian, and Bella Bella. There is no mention of xeroxing or making of transparencies, however all the activity sheets may be used in this manner for groups of children. Be sure to duplex pages needing drawings on both sides of paper.

All Indian people along the Northwest Coast use button blankets. This book shows the button blankets in the art style of the Kwakiutl.

For more information the following reference materials will be very helpful.

Boas, Franz
*"The Decorative Art of the Indians of the North Pacific Coast."* Bulletin of the American Museum of Natural History, New York, Vol. 9, 1987.

Holm, Bill
*Northwest coast Indian Art; An Analysis of Form,* University of Washington Press, Seattle, 1965.

Stewart, Hilary
*Looking at Indian Art of the Northwest Coast,* Douglas and McIntyre Ltd., Vancouver, B.C., 1979.

Jensen, Doreen and Polly Sargent
*"Robes of Power: Totem Poles On Cloth,"* U.B.C. Press, Vancouver, B.C., 1986.

Otness, Sharol
*The Tlingit Button Blanket."* Unpublished Master's Thesis, Oregon State University, Corvallis, Oregon, 1979.

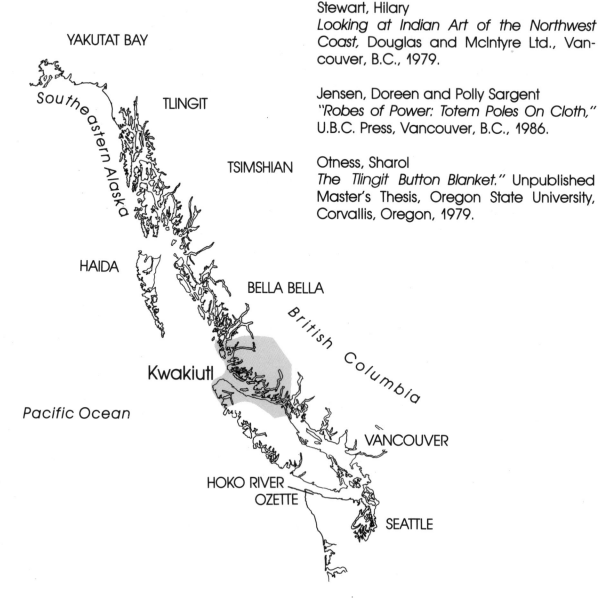

# More about the story:

Discuss these concepts with your children, then read the story again.

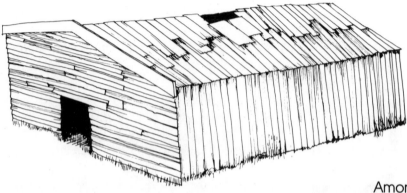

## Big Houses:

Today, Indian people live in Euro-American style houses. But in almost every town there is a community hall or a big house where community gatherings and potlatches are held.

Long ago Indian peoples lived in big houses. Kwakiutl houses could be as big as 80 feet long, 50 feet wide and 30 feet high. Everyone who lived in the house belonged to the same family. Children grew up with grandparents, aunts, uncles, cousins, parents and brothers and sisters.

## Crests:

Crests are animal-like designs that belong to certain families. They may represent an ancestor or special power. For these reasons only persons entitled to use a crest may do so.

In the story Ann receives her crest from her uncle.

Among the Kwakiutl people, a person inherits crests from both the mother's and the father's sides of the family. Among other peoples crests may come from only the father's side or mother's side.

## Potlatch:

When a family feels that it is the right time to publicly recognize its family's prerogatives, such as names, titles, social ranks and crests, a celebration is held. This celebration, called a potlatch, has feasting, dancing, and much gift giving. These gifts are a payment to the guests for recognizing the family prerogatives. The guests are invited from all over and are treated with respect, the host ever mindful of their social rank. It is a time for protocol yet there is lots of excitment in seeing old friends.

## Adze (ad'z):

One of the carving tools used by all NW Coast Indians is the adze. It is used by striking down towards oneself, taking off chips much as a chisel does.

Ann's uncle is using one to carve his frontlet which he wears on his head when he dances with his button blanket. He has added sealion whiskers on the top to hold eagle down and a train of white weasel or ermine pelts down the back. When he dances the white eagle down falls and floats around him. Quite often a Chilkat blanket (a woven robe of wool and cedar bark with complex crest designs) will be worn instead of a button blanket.

## Family:

Today as well as in the past Indian families are closely bound. It is very common to have grandparents, parents, aunts, uncles and cousins living in the same household. Ann's household family consists of her grandparents, parents, baby brother and uncle.

You might want to compare this household with your children's families.
1. How would you eat your meals?
2. Where would you all sleep?
3. Who would help you do your homework?
4. With whom would you play?

# To Make A Button Blanket

In the summer of 1980 archeologists excavating at the Hoko River site on the Olympic Peninsula in Washington found remnants of a blanket made of cedar bark. Its delicate twined fibers quickly turned dark brown as it became exposed to the air after 2000 years of being buried in wet clay.

Not far from the Hoko River site at the coastal Ozette village another type of blanket was excavated. This one, made of spun wool or dog hair, had been woven into a striking blue and white plaid pattern. It dated four hundred years old.

Ancient stories from every part of the Northwest Coast tell of women weaving blankets of mountain goat wool, dog's hair, cedar bark, strips of animal fur or feathers. Some of these types eventually gave way to the European trade blanket, but the Chilkat and Salish blankets are still being made today. Salish blankets are white woven dog or mountain goat wool robes.

The earliest records of trading for blankets date back to the 1740's. British, Spanish, Russian and American ships came to purchase sea otter pelts which they sold for high prices in China. Trade blankets remained a primary exchange item throughout the fur trade era. The fact remains, it was easier to trade furs for a blanket than to make one. One did not need to collect the material, prepare it, spin it, and then weave it. Trading was convenient and the blanket was just as functional. So important did commercial blankets become that by the mid 1800's they were the monetary standard. Wages were even paid in blankets.

## Ornaments:

Equally attractive to the Indians beginning in the earliest years of the fur trade were the new ornaments available to them: yellow brass uniform buttons, beads, small bells, Chinese coins, thimbles and mother of pearl buttons. These were attached to the blankets along with the traditional ornaments of native copper, abalone, and dentalium shell.

By the early 1800's a classic button blanket made of dark blue blanket and red trade cloth and embellished with mother of pearl buttons was fashioned. Among the Kwakiutl and groups to the north, it became an important ceremonial clothing and was worn at important gatherings to display an individual's crest.

## Group Activity:

There is nothing more wonderful than to experience something real. There is nothing better for the learning process than providing something real. Although most of your children will never get to go to an Indian potlatch you can give them some other real experiences.

Ask your children to find out if any of them have a button blanket at home. Perhaps their parents will bring it in and share it. If not, then sew one with your group of children. Traditionally all sewing was done by hand, as it was prior to the sewing machine. It's very possible that your children have never seen anyone sew by hand or even on a machine.

Ask some of your parents who have a machine and know how to sew, to volunteer to sew in the room during an activity period. It is important for them to see quality craftsmanship.

*WHAT YOU NEED:*
1½ YD OF DARK BLUE WOOL (blanket)
½ YD RED WOOL (border)
¼ YD RED COTTON (neck protection)
PINS & NEEDLE
SCISSORS
THREAD
MEASURING TAPE
IRON
SEWING MACHINE

# Activity:
## Button Blanket

## A. Establishing the length  of a blanket

1. Measure the child's back from middle of the neck to 2" above the ankle (back measurement).

2. Transfer this back measurement to the material beginning at one salvage end (finished edge). Mark the distance with pins in a number of places.

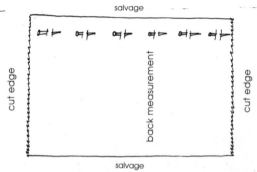

3. Fold the material along the pin line and cut along the fold.

## B. Establishing the 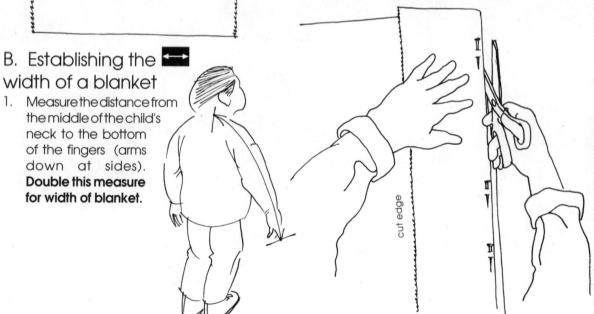 width of a blanket

1. Measure the distance from the middle of the child's neck to the bottom of the fingers (arms down at sides). **Double this measure for width of blanket.**

2. Transfer this doubled measurement to the material by beginning your measurement at one **cut** edge. Make sure that this cut edge is square to the salvage! Mark the distance with pins in a number of places.

3. Fold the material along the pin line and cut along the fold.

## C. The Border

**note: the wrong side of the material is shaded**

1. Cut the length of the red wool into 8 inch strips so that you have 3 long strips of material.

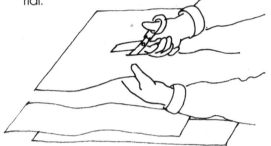

2. Sew these strips together. The total length must be equal or more than the total length of the blanket's top and two sides.

3. Fold this border strip in half (at the center of the middle strip) and mark the fold with a pin.

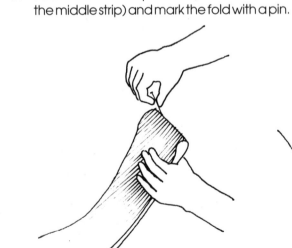

4. Attach the center of the border strip to the center of the blanket top (wrong sides out).

5. Pin border and blanket top together along the outer edge. Sew the border to the blanket, ¼ inch seam.

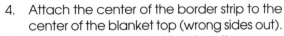
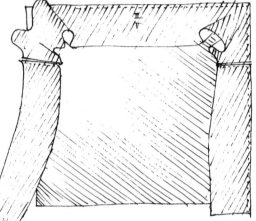

6. Now clip the corners to get rid of excess material.

7. To press the seams open, lay a damp (cotton) cloth over the open seam and press with iron (wool setting).

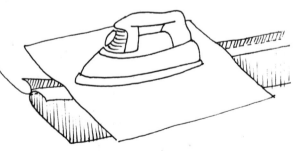

8. Fold the border over with the seam to the inside and press again with a damp cloth.

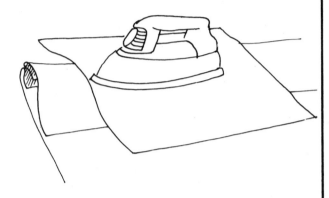

9. Fold the corners at a right angle, and press with damp cloth.

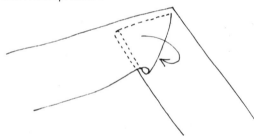

10. Hand sew the right angle fold to make a mitered corner, press again with a damp cloth.

11. Turn the raw edge of the border to the inside ¼ - ½", pin, and sew by hand.
Press lightly with damp cloth

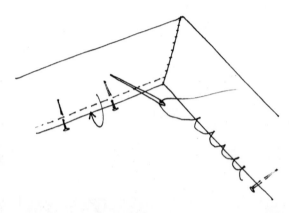

## Collar Protection

Generally to protect the wool around the neck, a piece of cotton material is attached. Both sides of the blanket are protected. This is placed in the middle of the border, where the back of the neck will rub.

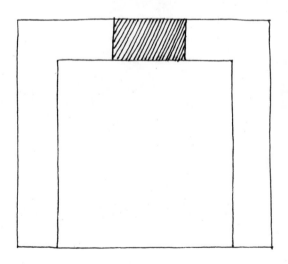

## Ties

**note: wrong side of material is shaded.**

1. With scrap material cut out 2 ties. They should be 1½ inch wide and 10 inches long.

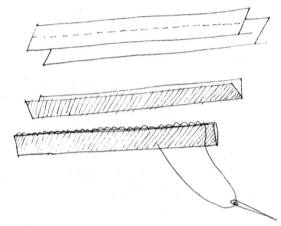

2. With right side together, fold & press length wise down middle and sew along length and one end.
3. Turn the strip inside out (You can use a wooden spoon handle). Press each tie.
4. Stitch the ends of the ties closed.

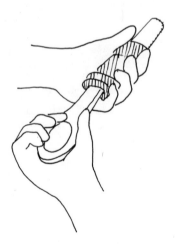

5. Attach the ties on the inside of the blanket. To find the spot. Rest the blanket on the shoulders and draw the blanket around the neck so that it touches at the front. This is the spot to attach the ties.

# Lesson 1

Classic Button Co.
P.O. Box 244
Bellevue, WA 98009
(206) 885-4518

The Legacy Ltd.
1003 1st Avenue
Seattle, WA 98104
(206) 624-6350

## The Buttons

All children love to count and sort buttons, and a thrift shop is an excellent source for them. Of course several containers or a cupcake tin will help in the sorting.

So that the children can see the difference between plastic buttons and mother of pearl or abalone buttons, purchase from a button company some shell buttons.

Your might also ask around for an abalone shell, preferably California abalone. Years before the European traders, Indians traded for these. They cut pieces from them and used them for ornaments, and they still do.

## Group Activity

*YOU NEED;*
2- ONE INCH MOTHER OF PEARL BUTTONS
JAR FULL OF BUTTONS (any kind)
PLASTIC TUBS OR CUPCAKE TINS

**If you want the buttons to hold onto the material, back them with velcro.**

1. Lay the button blanket out on the floor.
2. Have each child place buttons on the border of the blanket. Let them make all kinds of designs.
3. When finished stand back and admire the work.
4. Explain that perhaps later you will put buttons on the border and this is what it might look like.
5. Have the children compare the mother of pearl buttons to the plastic buttons.

# Lesson 2

Northwest Coast Indian art is a very old form dating back according to archaeological finds to at least 2,000 years ago. It is a precise art form, comprised of specific elements that when combined create a whole design.

The next time you visit a museum that displays traditional button blankets, pay particular attention to how the design is appliqued on the blanket. It is usually one piece that is made up of different shapes. The most frequent of these shapes will look like this ⌒ or ◼ called a U form and ▢ or ◼ called an ovoid.

## Group Activities

Because you will need to use the patterns on pages 17, 21, & 24 more than once, make copies of these for the children.

Because much learning is facilitated by feeling and doing, the following activities have been set up to maximize that learning style.

For the younger children use the patterns on pages 14 and 18 for making "feelies" out of felt board material, or sandpaper glued on flashcards. Some teachers have even used glitter. The more they feel these shapes, the more quickly they will be able to see them in complex designs.

*ADDITIONAL MATERIAL NEEDED:*
NEWSPAPER &
WASTE PAPER BASKET.

Put small amounts of glue on wax paper for each person. You may want to back the shapes with tag board or cardboard.

## Activity 1

1.
2. Pass out page 14.
3. Pass out small quantities of glue.

Have everyone, when they have spread the glue, come to a central location to sprinkle on salt or cornmeal. Have the area covered with newspaper with a waste paper bas-ket in the middle.

4. Let dry before allowing children to play with them.

## Activity II

1. Pass out pages 15 & 16.
2. Pass out scissors and have everyone cut the other U forms.
3. Ask the group to compare the two U forms. How are they the same? How are they different? What else can you tell me about U forms? If there is no response, take one U form and fold it in half. Allow the children to verbalize what they see in their own way.
4. Color the U"s. For younger children, this may be a good cutoff point.
5. Have the children trace their U forms on the

# Lesson 3

black board or separate sheets.

6. Pass out page 14 and paste.
7. Have everyone match up U's and paste them down.
8. Color the rest of the design.

## Activities III & IV

Proceed with pages 18 through 21, as done in preceding activities.

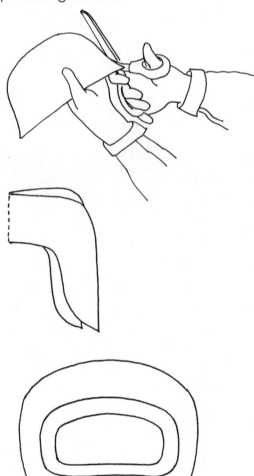

## Button Blanket Design

Today the button blanket and its traditions remain close to the Indian people. Certain customs dictate when and how the blanket may be used. These customs vary from one culture group to another.

Variations are also seen in the style of the blanket from one group to another. All blankets, however, have the same basic rectangle shape. A border trims three sides but not the bottom.

Different designs are used in the application of buttons near the border. The Kwakiutl people place the buttons in various patterns right on the border. (example)

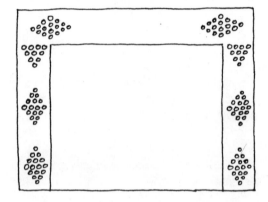

Northern people apply the buttons in rows along-side the border. Buttons were sewn on with a running stitch, not individually. (example)

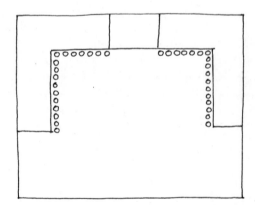

A crest design may or may not be sewn in the center of the back. This depends on whether the person has inherited the right to wear a crest and has paid for the privilege of wearing it.

The felt or wool appliqued crest is embellished with buttons, but there is variation. Among the Tlingit the applique is sometimes left off entirely and only buttons or beads are used to depict the crest.

Among the Kwakiutl, green can be used as the basic blanket color. Button blankets among the Bella Bella and Bella Coola sometimes follow the northern style and sometimes the Kwakiutl style.

The only button blankets that do not follow this general style came from the Tlingits. These are "crosswise over the shoulders," depicted in illustration (a). And "Four Stripe" and shown in illustration (b).

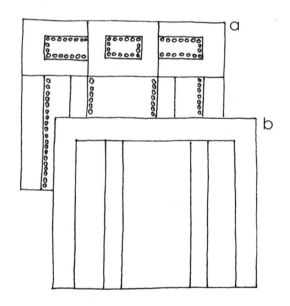

The Coast Salish people never developed the button blanket, although they used trade blankets for everyday use. For their ceremonies they continued into the mid 1900's to weave their mountain goat wool blankets. This was more a factor of religious values than function. Today, however, at a party you may see people wearing button blankets as an adapted tradition from the north.

## Group Activities
*ADDITIONAL MATERIALS NEEDED:*
P. 21 or 23, 24
GLUE ON WAX PAPER FOR EACH PERSON
TINY BUTTONS, SEQUINS, GLITTER, AND/OR
SIGNAL BUTTONS
BACKPACK DESIGN SEE #8

## Activity I
1.  Have everyone cut out their puzzle pieces.
2.  Put the puzzle together.
3.  Have the children glue the pieces of puzzle while they are together as a puzzle.
4.  Now they can apply them to blue construction paper one piece at a time.
5.  Pass out a button to each person to glue as an eye.
6.  Older children may want to sew their button down. Make sure they glue the edge of the button, not the middle.
7.  You may want to use sequins, glitter, signal dots, or tiny buttons for trim and design.
8.  For a backpack design, cut the puzzle pieces out of cloth (by adult). Then have the child glue the pieces to a backpack.

## Activity II
*ADDITIONAL MATERIALS NEEDED;*
THREAD PLASTIC YARN NEEDLE and BUTTON BLANKET YOU ARE MAKING WITH THE GROUP

Thread the needles and buttons prior to doing the activity. It might be wise to do some extras in case of a mistake. The following method of threading will make the sewing less frustrating for everyone.

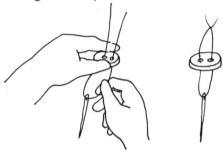

When children sew, the knot stays on top of the button, and the needle will not slip off the thread.

1.  If you or another adult have not done so already demonstrate to the group how to sew on buttons. As you sew repeat the words "down," "up," "down," "up," and have the children imitate your movement.
2.  Show where to place the eye button.
3.  Pass out a threaded button and needle as well as their button blanket design.
4.  Have the children sew on an eye. (button)

## Activity III
## The Whale Pattern
(parent supervision required)

*ADDITIONAL MATERIALS NEEDED:*
COPIES OF PAGES 17 (TWO SETS),
21, AND 23
LARGE BUTCHER OR NEWSPRINT PAPER
½ YD RED FELT
1 LARGE BUTTON FOR EYE
OPTIONAL: BUTTONS FOR BODY

## Head and Tail

1. Cut out the whale's head and tail. Discard the background spaces.
2. Lay these out on your finished blanket. The position is up to you. (example)

3. Transfer the head and tail onto a sheet of butcher paper in the same position and spacing.
4. Lightly sketch the outline of the whale's body connecting the head and the tail (lines a & b). Don't worry about the fin and flippers.
5. If you like what you have designed, paste down the head and tail.

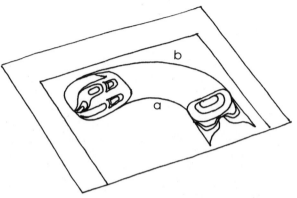

## Dorsal Fin

1. Cut out one set of "U"s (p. 17). Discard the background space between the "U"s.

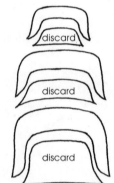

2. Place the stack of "U"s on the top of the whale's back (straight up or bent). Check height on the blanket.
3. If you bend the fin, stretch or trim the legs of the "U"s so that they connect and blend in smoothly to the "U" they sit upon.

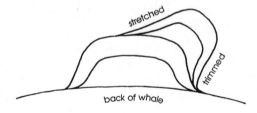

4. If you like your design, paste the dorsal fin into place.

## Flipper

1. Cut out the second stack of "U"s.
2. The points of each leg of the largest "U" touch the back of the jaw.
3. Place the "U"s bent or straight.
4. If you like your design, paste down the flipper.

## Body

1. Draw two more lines to complete the body.
2. Notice in the illustration below that the lines are equal distant until they taper as they connect with head and tail. Taper these lines.

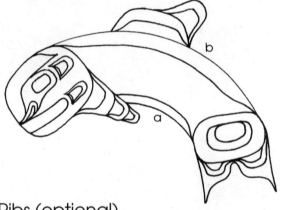

## Ribs (optional)

1. To fill in the body cavity a third design element, called a "S", is used to form the ribs. Important: In the illustration below the ribs should be red, not the blue background. They look like "S"s or "Z"s depending on the direction they face.

# Lesson 4

2. Using the illustration below as a guide, draw the ribs in free hand since each one fits into a different space.

## The Whale Applique

1. Before you cut out your pattern, color all the body parts red, so it will be easier to reassemble the design.
2. Cut out the pattern and pin it on the red felt.
3. Cut out the felt and with glue lightly tacking it to the blanket.
4. Hand sew the crest design on to the blanket. Optional: sew on buttons or sequins where desired. Perhaps even as the whale's spout. (see illustration above)

## Music and Movement

Now that you have a completed button blanket, have the children try it on. They will experience the weight, the warmth and the movement.

A record of Kwakiutl music has been put out by *Folkway's Ethnic Library*, and if your library or school district Indian education office does not have it, a record store can order it.

INDIAN MUSIC OF THE PACIFIC NORTHWEST COAST RECORD: FOLKWAYS ETHNIC LIBRARY
FE4523-KWAKIUTL
FE 4119-HAIDA
   FOLKWAYS RECORDS & SERVICE CORP.
   632 BROADWAY
   NY, NY 10012

KWAKIUTL SONGS AND VIDEO
   U'MISTA CULTURE CENTER
   P.O. BOX 253
   ALERT BAY, B.C., CANADA   VON IAO

Most of this music will not sound familiar. First have the children listen to the music and beat out a rhythm to become accustom to it.

Explain that these songs are different from our songs in two ways.

1. They are highly stylized with parts of words being repeated.

2. All songs are owned and only the owner and heirs have the right to sing and dance them. However, your children can learn and experience the basic movement.

## Group Activity
## Basic Moves

### Bouncing
1. Explain to the children that the blanket's crest needs to be displayed while a dancer is dancing.
2. Have the children place their hands on their hips to see how the crest on the back of the blanket can best be seen.
3. With hands on hips, have the children stand with their feet apart and knees bent.
4. Bounce to the beat of the music.

### Turning
1. With hands in the same position as above, slowly turn one way and then another with the music.
2. Continue bouncing while turning feet, shoulders and head.

### Walking
1. Again in the same position, step to the music slowly turning first one way and then another.
2. Make up a circle dance. Have the children go around in a circle stopping to bounce with feet on floor, then with feet coming off floor, and then back to walking.

# Lesson 5

## Dancing Paper Persons
## Group Activities

*ADDITIONAL MATERIALS NEEDED:*
COPIES OF PAGES 26 AND 27 OR 28.
COVER OF BOOK
   Option: Order Button Blanket Sheets. (see end of book)
4 WIRE COAT HANGERS
TAPE (HEAVY DUTY)
WIRE CLIPPERS
GLUE ON WAX PAPER FOR EACH PERSON

These additional materials are for a mobile on which to hang the paper persons.

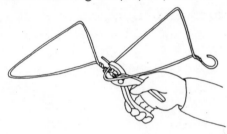

Pinch the hook on one hanger over the bottom wire of another hanger, as shown in the drawing. Make sure it is balanced and then secure its position with tape. Have this prepared before doing the activities.

Also make a model of a paper person and a button blanket, so everyone understands what the activity is about. If you are working with younger children, cut away excess paper from around the figure and blanket parts so that it is not too difficult for them to handle. Or for those who have not learned to handle scissors, you may wish to cut out all the blanket pieces in the beginning.

## Activity I

1. Pass out pages 26 and 27 or 28 to each person. Look at the instructions.
2. Have everyone color an image of themselves on the figure. Each person may dress themselves as they would like. The figure is only a pattern. Remember there is the backside, too.
3. Now pass out scissors and have the children cut out the paper person.
4. Attach paper clip with tape where indicated and tie a string to the paper clip.
5. Now tie the other end of the string to the mobile. Secure with tape. Remember to balance the paper persons by alternating from one side and then the other.

## Activity II

1. Pass out the paper button blanket on the cover or from The Button Blanket Sheet and pages 26.
2. Fold the sheet according to instructions on page 26. Be sure that each fold is folded on itself so that it is flexible in both directions.
3. Place the blankets over the shoulders of the paper person, tape and let the whole group dance in the wind.

# The Northwest Coast Indian Art Activity Books

## Nan McNutt

This series of fun activity books features the art and culture of Native Americans from Northwest Coastal areas—including the Tlingit, Haida, Tsimshian, Bella Bella, Kwakiutl, and Salish. Each book is reviewed for cultural accuracy by tribal members and uses the work of Northwest Native artists. Activities are field-tested in classrooms, and each volume provides an Adult Teaching Guide. Ages 6-10.

### Also of interest—A great resource for Northwest Native culture and travel!

*Native Peoples of the Northwest: A Traveler's Guide to Land, Art, & Culture*

Jan Halliday and Gail Chehak

In cooperation with the Affiliated Tribes of Northwest Indians

**SASQUATCH BOOKS**
SEATTLE

Nan McNutt
& Associates

Available at bookstores or order from Sasquatch Books, below:

| | qty | $ |
|---|---|---|
| *The Bentwood Box*, ISBN 1-57061-116-5, 36 pp, $10.95 | _____ | _____ |
| *The Button Blanket*, ISBN 1-57061-118-1, 44 pp, $10.95 | _____ | _____ |
| *The Cedar Plank Mask*, ISBN 1-57061-117-3, 36 pp, $10.95 | _____ | _____ |
| *The Spindle Whorl*, ISBN 1-57061-115-7, 44pp, $10.95 | _____ | _____ |
| *Native Peoples of the Northwest*, ISBN 1-57061-056-8, 256 pp, $16.95 | _____ | _____ |
| Subtotal | _____ | _____ |
| Tax (WA residents only; add 8.6%) | | _____ |
| Shipping ($4 for first book, $1 for each additional) | | _____ |
| TOTAL | | _____ |

SHIP TO: Name_____ Address_____

City_____ State_____ Zip_____ Phone_____

☐ Check/Money Order enclosed  ☐ Visa  ☐ Mastercard  Account #_____ Exp date_____

Signature _____ Printed name _____ Phone_____

Send order to: Sasquatch Books, 615 Second Ave., Ste. 260, Seattle, WA 98104    (206) 467-4300; Fax (206) 467-4301; Email: books@sasquatchbooks.com

### Or call TOLL-FREE: (800) 775-0817 — Ask for a free catalog of all our Northwest, children's, and Native American titles!